Welcoming the Presence
of the Spirit

D1466534

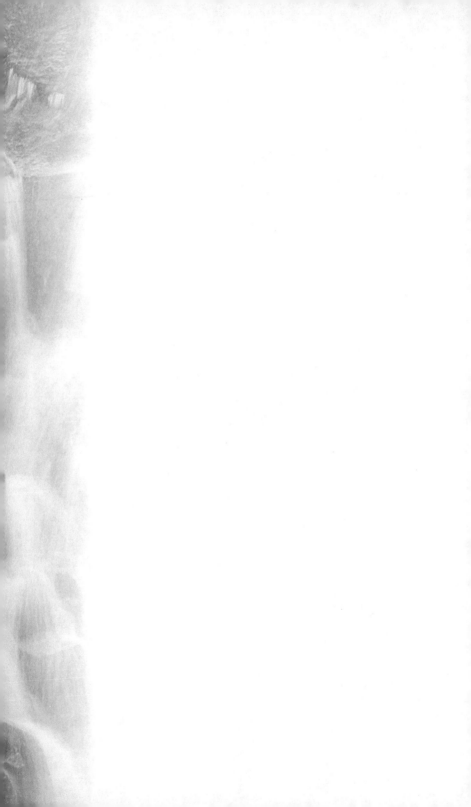

VOLUME 1

Welcoming *the* Presence *of the* Spirit

Do not stifle the Holy Spirit.
1 Thessalonians 5:19

**A 30-day Devotional Bible Study
for Individuals or Groups.**

Dr. Larry Keefauver

Charisma®
HOUSE
Books about Spirit-Led Living

WELCOMING THE PRESENCE OF THE SPIRIT by Larry Keefauver

Published by Charisma House
A part of Strang Communications Company
600 Rinehart Road
Lake Mary, FL 32746

www.charismahouse.com

Unless otherwise noted, all Scripture quotations are the Holy Bible, New Living Translation, copyright © 1996. Used by permission of Tyndale House Publishers, Inc., Wheaton, IL 60189. All rights reserved.

01 02 03 04   11 10 9 8 7

Contents

Introduction

Welcome to this devotional study guide on welcoming the Holy Spirit into your life. This is one of eight devotional studies related to the *Holy Spirit Encounter Bible.* While it is not necessary, it is suggested that you obtain a copy of the *Holy Spirit Encounter Bible* for your personal use with this study guide. The translation used in this guide is the *New Living Translation,* which is also the translation for the *Holy Spirit Encounter Bible.*

Do not feel that you must go through this devotional series in any particular order. Choose the guides and order that best meet your spiritual needs.

This devotional study guide may be used by individuals, groups, or classes. Four guides for group or class sessions are at the end of this devotional study for those using this guide in a group setting. Groups using this guide should complete their devotional studies prior to their group sessions. This will greatly enhance sharing, studying, and praying together.

Individuals going through this guide can use it for daily devotional reading and study. The purpose of this guide is to help the reader(s) encounter the person of the Holy Spirit through the Scriptures. Each daily devotional study is structured to:

❖ Probe deeply into the Scriptures.

❖ Examine one's own personal relationship with the Holy Spirit.

❖ Discover biblical truths about the Holy Spirit.

❖ Encounter the person of the Holy Spirit continually in one's daily walk with God.

We pray that this study guide will be an effective tool for equipping you to study God's Word and to encounter the wonderful third person of the Triune God, the Holy Spirit.

*A*nd so I tell you, keep on asking, and you will be given what you ask for. Keep on looking, and you will find. Keep on knocking, and the door will be opened. For everyone who asks, receives. Everyone who seeks, finds. And the door is opened to everyone who knocks. You fathers—if your children ask for a fish, do you give them a snake instead? Or if they ask for an egg, do you give them a scorpion? Of course not! If you sinful people know how to give good gifts to your children, how much more will your heavenly Father give the Holy Spirit to those who ask him (Luke 11:9–13).

DAY 1

Ask for the Holy Spirit

God gives the Holy Spirit to those who ask. Too often we ask God for things *from Him* instead of simply asking Him to give *of Himself.*

Think about your requests of the heavenly Father. Make a list of your most recent prayer requests:

1. _____

2. _____

3. _____

4. _____

5. _____

Now examine your list. Put a check by each item that is stuff. Put an *x* by each item that is for another person. Now circle each item that simply requests more of the Lord—i.e., desiring a deeper or more intimate relationship with God through His Spirit.

Jesus commands us, "Take my yoke upon you. Let me teach you, because I am humble and gentle, and you will find rest for your souls" (Matt. 11:29). How does He teach us about Himself? How does God reveal Himself to us?

Read these verses and jot down a brief summary of how we learn of Jesus:

John 14:26 _____

_____

John 15:26 _____

_____

John 16:15 _____

_____

Asking the Father for things will never satisfy our heart's deepest hunger—to *know* Him. Read Psalms 42:1–2 and 46:10. Put an *x* on the line marking how intensely you desire and hunger after God's Spirit:

_____

Very intense   Apathetic

> *When we ask the Father for the Holy Spirit and receive His Spirit, we discover anew that in His Spirit every other need that we have is met.*

God the Father desires to give you His Holy Spirit. The gift of His Spirit comes when you trust Jesus Christ as your personal Lord and Savior. In the coming days, you will discover how to receive the gift of the Holy Spirit.

Ask yourself . . .

❖ Do I desire more *of* God or simply more *from* Him?

❖ Am I truly hungering and thirsting after God?

❖ Is my greatest need a gift from the Giver or the Giver Himself?

Write a prayer asking God for His Holy Spirit:

_____

_____

_____

_____

_____

*J*esus replied, "The truth is, no one can enter the Kingdom of God without being born of water and the Spirit" (John 3:5).

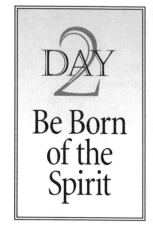

DAY 2
Be Born of the Spirit

Some people ask, "Is there life after death?" Before answering this profound question, we must first answer another question: "Is there life after *birth?*"

After natural birth, a person merely exists. True life can only be found in Jesus Christ, "I [Jesus] am the way, the truth, and the life. No one can come to the Father except through me" (John 14:6). Existence ceases and life begins when a person receives Jesus Christ as Lord and Savior. "What this means is that those who become Christians become new persons. They are not the same anymore, for the old life [existence] is gone. A new life has begun!" (2 Cor. 5:17).

This new life in Jesus Christ is often referred to as "being born again." Our first birth was natural. Our second (spiritual) birth through faith in Jesus Christ is supernatural.

> *Before persons can encounter the presence of God's Spirit, they must first be born of water and the Spirit.*

Look up each Scripture and put it in the correct column: Matthew 28:19; Acts 2:38; Romans 6:1–11; Romans 8:9–11; 2 Corinthians 3:1–6; 1 Corinthians 6:11; Ephesians 5:25–26; Titus 3; Mark 16:16; Acts 8:12; 1 Corinthians 12:13; Colossians 2:12; 1 Peter 2:23; John 3:7; John 3:8; 1 Peter 1:3; Galatians 4:29.

Born of Water	**Born of the Spirit**
_____	_____
_____	_____
_____	_____
_____	_____
_____	_____
_____	_____
_____	_____

When we repent of our sins and confess Jesus Christ as Lord and Savior, we submit ourselves in obedience to water baptism as Jesus commanded (Matt. 28:19). Inwardly, the blood of Jesus Christ cleanses us from all sin (1 John 1:9). Jesus shed His blood and died on the cross for our sin. Read Isaiah 53 and Romans 3 and 5.

Around the cross below, write down some of the sins in your life that Jesus died for and washed away by His blood.

When we are born again, we receive the gift of the Holy Spirit in our lives (Acts 2:38). If you have never repented and confessed Jesus Christ as your Lord and Savior, pray this: (And if you have confessed Christ, then pray it again as a rededication.)

Jesus, I repent of my sins and ask You to forgive me. I confess that You are the Son of the living God, the Christ, and I receive You as my personal Lord and Savior. Thank You for shedding Your blood and forgiving my sins so that I might have the gift of eternal life. Amen.

*P*eter replied, "Each of you must turn from your sins and turn to God, and be baptized in the name of Jesus Christ for the forgiveness of your sins. Then you will receive the gift of the Holy Spirit" (Acts 2:38).

We must first repent of our sins. In obedience, we are baptized in the name of Jesus Christ, whose shed blood has forgiven us of our sins. Then we receive the gift of the Holy Spirit. We do nothing to earn this free gift!

> *The gift of the Holy Spirit brings into our lives the awesome presence of God's Spirit.*

Receive the Gift of the Holy Spirit

The Spirit's work of sanctifying us—making us pure and holy—begins within us.

These Scriptures overview some of the wonderful benefits of the gift of the Holy Spirit in our lives. Read each passage and then, in a word or phrase, list on the present below how the gift of the Holy Spirit is at work in our lives: Matthew 3:11; 10:20; John 7:38–39; Acts 1:8; 2:4; 2:17; Romans 8:11; 8:26–27; 1 Corinthians 2:10–14; 6:19; 2 Corinthians 3:18; Ephesians 4:4; 1 John 4:1–4.

Now look over what you wrote down. Circle each way in which you have already encountered the Holy Spirit in your life. Underline every way that you would like to encounter.

People may be afraid of receiving all the benefits of the gift of the Spirit at work within them. If you have not experienced the fullness of God's Spirit at work in you, what has hindered you? Check everything that hinders the gift of the Holy Spirit from being fully at work within you:

❏ Fear of losing control.

❏ Not knowing all His benefits.

❏ Afraid of losing control of my life.

❏ Unconfessed sin or unbroken bondages in my life.

❏ Lack of hunger for the Spirit.

❏ Fearful of the opinions of others.

As you study each subject in this devotional, you will grow in your understanding of how the gift of God's Spirit is at work in your life. On each line below, mark where you are now in your encounter with the Holy Spirit:

I know I have the gift
of the Holy Spirit.

I am unsure about
the gift of the Spirit.

I desire everything the Spirit
has for me in my life.

I am uncertain about
the Holy Spirit.

Write a prayer thanking God for the gift of the Holy Spirit.

B ut when the Holy Spirit has come upon you, you will receive power and will tell people about me everywhere—in Jerusalem, throughout Judea, in Samaria, and to the ends of the earth (Acts 1:8).

The power *(dunamis)* of the Holy Spirit refers to the miracle-working, supernatural force of God imparted to us by the presence of His Holy Spirit in our lives.

The Holy Spirit's power can be encountered in many different ways, but the first way His power is revealed is in the saving power of the gospel.

Read Romans 1:16–17 and then rewrite or paraphrase the verses in your own words.

DAY 4
Receive the Power

_____

_____

_____

_____

> *The Spirit's power eradicates all timidity and shame as you witness about Christ to others.*

No longer will you fear what others think about you. Your boldness in witnessing comes from the power of the Holy Spirit. Gauge the power of His boldness in your witnessing. On the graph below, shade up to your level of witnessing:

	Family	Friends	Strangers	Enemies
Extreme boldness				
Courageous				
Not afraid				
Cautious				
Ashamed/afraid				

The awesome power of God's Spirit that raised Jesus from the dead lives within every believer (Rom. 8:11). Through the Spirit's power you have the ability to witness, to work mighty signs, wonders, and miracles, and to live victoriously for Christ. With the Spirit's ability must come your availability to be used by Him. Are you available?

Right now, where do you most need to experience the Spirit's power? Place a check in the boxes that indicate areas where you need the Spirit's power to be applied:

❑ Friendships   ❑ Marriage

❑ Family   ❑ Workplace

❑ Finances   ❑ Health

❑ Church   ❑ Breaking bondages

❑ Witnessing   ❑ Ministering to others

❑ Other: _____

Write a prayer asking God to fill you with the Spirit's mighty, miracle-working power:

_____

_____

_____

_____

_____

*T*hen he [Jesus] breathed on them and said to them, "Receive the Holy Spirit" (John 20:22).

The first Adam received life from the breath of God: "And the Lord God formed a man's body from the dust of the ground and breathed into it the breath of life. And the man became a living person" (Gen. 2:7). Throughout Scripture, the breath or wind of God is His Spirit. In fact, the Hebrew word *ru'ach*—which is translated Spirit, for God's Spirit—literally means "breath or wind."

However, Adam sinned, and the life of God's breath that had sustained him departed, leaving him and his descendants cursed to die. But now the second Adam—Jesus Christ—breathes the Holy Spirit of life upon His disciples. A new race of humanity is being birthed by the Spirit of God. No longer under the curse of death which was broken on the cross by Christ (Gal. 3:10–14), the life we live is by the power of the Holy Spirit.

> We have eternal life through the breath of God's Spirit, imparted to us by our Savior, Jesus Christ.

Receiving the gift of the Spirit from Christ is receiving the fullness of life. Look at some of the wonderful promises Jesus made about the life He gives by the Spirit: Jot down a brief summary of the promise in each verse.

John 3:16 _____

John 4:10–14 _____

John 7:38–39 _____

John 6:35–40, 63 _____

John 10:10 _____

John 11:25–26 _____

John 14:6–7 _____

Life in the Spirit is described throughout Romans 8. Draw a line matching our life in the Spirit with the promise reference from Romans, chapter eight:

Life in the Spirit	Match to a Promise
Romans 8:1	Adopted by God the Father
Romans 8:3	Overwhelming victory
Romans 8:5	Thoughts that please God
Romans 8:6	No condemnation
Romans 8:9	Raised from the dead
Romans 8:10	Sin's control destroyed
Romans 8:11	No separation from God
Romans 8:13	Alive in our spirit
Romans 8:23	Life and peace
Romans 8:26	The Spirit prays for us
Romans 8:28	A foretaste of glory
Romans 8:37	Controlled by the Spirit
Romans 8:38	God causes everything to work together for good

In the first Adam, all died. But now in Christ, the second Adam, all are made alive by the Spirit of God that raised Him from the dead. Paul writes in Romans 5:17, "The sin of this one man, Adam, caused death to rule over us, but all who receive God's wonderful, gracious gift of righteousness will live in triumph over sin and death through this one man, Jesus."

Receiving life through Jesus' breath, how will you praise and thank Him? Complete these sentences:

Jesus, I thank You for_____.

Jesus, breathe Your Spirit on me that I may _____.

Write a prayer asking Jesus to breathe upon you with the breath of His Spirit:

_____

_____

_____

*I*f you love me, obey my commandments. And I [Jesus] will ask the Father, and he will give you another Counselor [Paraclete], who will never leave you (John 14:15–16).

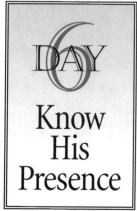

DAY 6

Know His Presence

Jesus promised His disciples that once He returned to His father, He would send a *paraclete*—which means "one who comforts, advocates, encourages, and counsels." Literally, the Holy Spirit as our *paraclete* "stands along side of us." He is always with us fulfilling the promise of the Father: "I will never fail you. I will never forsake you" (Heb. 13:5; Deut. 31:6).

The Holy Spirit also fulfills the promise of Jesus: "And be sure of this: I am with you always, even to the end of the age" (Matt. 28:20).

Another name for the *paraclete* is helper.

> *The Holy Spirit helps us live holy, pure lives in every area of our thoughts, feelings, attitudes, and actions.*

Notice that the Holy Spirit is a person just as are the Father and the Son. He is the third person of the Trinity. We have a personal relationship with the Spirit because our triune God is a personal God desiring a close, intimate relationship with us.

Each personal characteristic of the Spirit is parallelled in the triune nature of God Himself. Read the following scriptures and check which attribute of God's nature is revealed:

God the Spirit Is:	Helper	Counselor	Comforter
Isaiah 9:6	❑	❑	❑
Psalm 54:4	❑	❑	❑
2 Corinthians 1:3	❑	❑	❑
Hebrews 13:6	❑	❑	❑
Isaiah 11:2	❑	❑	❑
Isaiah 12:1	❑	❑	❑
Psalm 145:14	❑	❑	❑

This brief overview of Scripture simply illustrates that the Holy Spirit is God's presence with us to comfort, help, and counsel us. The Spirit's nature is the same nature as that of the Father and the Son. So whatever the Spirit does in our lives is the work of the Father and the Son in us as well.

God's Spirit is present and with us in every moment. The presence of His Spirit is beautifully expressed in Psalm 139:7–12. Read the following passage aloud. Put your own name in place of the personal pronoun, "I." <u>Underline</u> the phrase or verse that means the most to you.

> *I can never escape from your spirit!*
> *I can never get away from your presence!*
> *If I go up to heaven, you are there;*
> *if I go down to the place of the dead, you are there.*
> *If I ride the wings of the morning—*
> *if I dwell by the farthest oceans*
> *even there your hand will guide me—*
> *and your strength will support me.*
> *I could ask the darkness to hide me*
> *and the light around me to become night—*
> *but even in darkness I cannot hide from you.*
> *To you the night shines as bright as day.*
> *Darkness and light are both alike to you.*
> *Psalm 139:7–12*

Write a prayer seeking the Spirit's presence at all times in your life:

_____

_____

_____

_____

_____

*B*ut when the Father sends the Counselor as my representative—and by the Counselor I mean the Holy Spirit—he will teach you everything and will remind you of everything I myself have told you (John 14:26).

DAY 7

Experience the Spirit's Comfort, Encouragement, and Counsel

There is wonderful comfort, encouragement, and counsel in truth. We can always rely on the Spirit to tell us the truth even when that truth may be personally painful. Why is that a comfort? Because He always speaks the truth in love. His truth always builds us up and never condemns us. The Spirit's encouragement never flatters us, but always affirms our strengths and even bolsters our weaknesses with His strength (2 Cor. 12:9).

Describe:

One way the Spirit comforts you: _____

_____

One way the Spirit encourages you: _____

_____

One way the Spirit counsels you: _____

_____

All these attributes of the Spirit fit perfectly with truth. Truth is absolute and unchanging. Truth is what is true for all people, at all times, and in all circumstances. Isn't it comforting to know that God's Spirit will be there today and tomorrow, no matter how miserably we might fail or sin?

Here are some areas of life in which you may need the Spirit's counsel, comfort, or encouragement. Put an *x* on the line for where you are right now:

_____

I need comfort from the Spirit.   I feel comforted.

_____

I need encouragement in my work.   I'm okay at work.

_____

I need counsel for a serious problem.   God is in control.

The Holy Spirit indwells His people (1 Cor. 3:16). This results in the Spirit using others to comfort, encourage, and counsel us.

List the people who minister the presence of His Spirit in your life:

The Holy Spirit uses _____ to encourage me.

The Holy Spirit uses _____ to counsel me.

The Holy Spirit uses _____ to comfort me.

The Holy Spirit also wishes to minister His presence through you to others. Complete these sentences with the names of those who come to mind:

_____ needs the encouragement of the Holy Spirit through me.

_____ needs the comfort of the Holy Spirit through me.

_____ needs the counsel of the Holy Spirit through me.

What you receive from the Holy Spirit, you can give to others. The more you give of the Spirit, the more you will be filled with His comfort, encouragement, and counsel.

Write a prayer asking for the Spirit to comfort, encourage, and counsel you:

_____

_____

_____

_____

_____

He is the Holy Spirit, who leads into all truth. The world at large cannot receive him, because it isn't looking for him and doesn't recognize him. But you do, because he lives with you now and later will be in you. . . . When the Spirit of truth comes, he will guide you into all truth (John 14:17; 16:13).

DAY 8

The Spirit of Truth Guides and Leads

The Holy Spirit guides us in all truth. He uses God's Word to lead and direct our way (John 16:13). As we hide the Word of God in our hearts (Ps. 119:11), the Holy Spirit uses that Word to be the truth (Num. 11:23; Ps. 33:4; Prov. 30:5; James 1:18) that directs our every thought and action (2 Tim. 3:16; Ps. 119:105).

The Word of God is the sword of the Spirit (Eph. 6:17). Look up each of the following verses and jot down how the sword of the Spirit—God's Word—guides us in each instance:

2 Timothy 3:16 _____

Hebrews 4:12–13 _____

Psalm 119:9–16 _____

Psalm 56 _____

Psalm 119:105–133 _____

John 17:13–17 _____

How can we hear and receive the Spirit's guidance in our lives? He directs us through various means. Here is a list of some of the means He uses to guide us. Check each way He has led you in the past:

❑ Through Scripture

❑ Through worship

❑ Through prayer

❑ Through prophecy

❑ Through the gifts of wisdom and knowledge

❑ Through dreams and visions

❑ Through the wise counsel of other believers

❑ Other: _____

Whenever the Holy Spirit guides us, He lifts up Jesus Christ and His will for our lives (John 16:12–15; 1 John 4:1–6). As He leads, comfort, peace, and encouragement fill our lives.

The Holy Spirit may lead us through difficult situations (Matt. 4:1), but He never guides us into temptation that is greater than we can resist or find a way through with His help (1 Cor. 10:13). Wherever He leads, He also prepares, strengthens, and equips us to go (2 Cor. 3:3, 5:5). And whatever trials we may face, He will help strengthen and refine our faith (1 Peter 1).

Describe a time in your life when the Holy Spirit guided you through and strengthened you in the face of difficulties:

_____

_____

_____

Write a prayer seeking the Spirit's guidance and direction:

_____

_____

_____

_____

_____

*B*ut when the Father sends the Counselor as my representative—and by the Counselor I mean Holy Spirit—he will teach you everything and will remind you of everything I myself have told you (John 14:26).

When the Holy Spirit teaches us, He imparts both knowledge and understanding. *Knowing* the truth needs to be coupled with *understanding* the truth. Knowledge recognizes facts, reality, and truth. But understanding applies knowledge in a practical, workable way to daily life.

The Holy Spirit helps us put our knowledge of the truth to work with understanding. Teaching is more than a skill; it is a gift of the Spirit (Rom. 12:7).

DAY 9

Be Taught by the Spirit

The Spirit both teaches us Himself and imparts His power and wisdom to others who can then teach us God's truth.

Sometimes the Spirit teaches us through Spirit-filled teachers who have the gift of teaching. And at other times, the Holy Spirit speaks to us directly as He teaches, instructs, and interprets God's truth to us.

Read the following passages and then jot down what they reveal about the Spirit teaching us:

Psalm 143:10 _____

Luke 12:12 _____

John 14:26 _____

1 John 2:27 _____

Since the Holy Spirit is also the spirit of wisdom (Isa. 11:2), He can teach us both what God says and what God means. The Spirit helps us see reality from God's perspective. Without the Spirit teaching us, we have eyes that do not see and ears that do not hear (Matt. 13:15). We need the Spirit to teach us spiritual truths so that we can understand and apply God's Word in our daily lives. So John writes, "But you have received the Holy Spirit, and he lives within you, so you don't need anyone to teach you what is true. For the Spirit teaches you all things, and what he teaches is true—it is not a lie. So continue in what he has taught you, and continue to live in Christ" (1 John 2:27).

Are you a willing and receptive student of the Holy Spirit? Below is a list of different areas of life. Mark those that apply to you with an *x* on the line to indicate where you are in that area:

When the Spirit teaches me in this area of my life, I am:

	An Eager Learner	A Poor Learner
Family life		
Marriage		
Parenting		
Church		
Biblical doctrine		
Work ethics		
Playing sports		
Use of language		
Use of spending money		
Loving my enemies		

Consider this warning if you marked the lines on the right side too many times: "This is why the Holy Spirit says, 'Today you must listen to his [God's] voice. Don't harden your hearts against him'" (Heb. 3:7–8).

Write a prayer asking the Holy Spirit to teach you in all truth:

_____

_____

_____

_____

_____

*L*et the words of Christ in all their richness live in your hearts and make you wise (Col. 3:16).

Have you ever forgotten something? It was right on the tip of your tongue. Yet, you simply could not recall what you knew so well but forgot so quickly.

How easy it is to forget even important things. But the Holy Spirit knows that about us. He helps us remember God's Word. He not only brings to mind the Word, but He also helps us remember just the right word for the specific needs and problems that we have.

DAY 10
Be Reminded of the Word By the Spirit

In order for the Spirit to remind us, there must first be something deposited in our hearts. That something is His Word. The Spirit cannot use what is not there. Read each of the following scriptures and write down how each verse says we can deposit God's Word into our lives:

Deuteronomy 31:11_____

Joshua 1:8 _____

Psalm 119:9 _____

Psalm 119:11 _____

Matthew 13:21–23 _____

Acts 6:4_____

Ephesians 6:17–18 _____

Philippians 2:16 _____

The Holy Spirit reminds us of God's Word for us in every situation of life.

In times of distress, the Spirit reminds us of His comforting words. In time of victory, the Spirit brings to mind His words of praise. First, we deposit His Word into our hearts. Then, we trust His Word brought to mind by His Spirit as we face decisions and choices at every turn in life's road. By His Word, the Spirit of God guides us in every step we take.

What Scriptures are brought to mind by the Holy Spirit at the following times in your life? Jot down a favorite Scripture that the Spirit reminds you of when . . .

❖ You are sad _____

❖ You rejoice _____

❖ You doubt _____

❖ You are confused _____

❖ You need hope _____

❖ You sin _____

❖ You hurt _____

❖ You seek God _____

Write a prayer asking the Holy Spirit to bring to remembrance His Word at all times:

_____

_____

_____

_____

_____

I f your sinful nature controls your mind, there is death. But if the Holy Spirit controls your mind, there is life and peace (Rom. 8:6).

DAY 11

Be Filled With His Peace

God's Spirit brings peace to a troubled mind. What is peace? In Hebrew, *shalom* means much more than simply the cessation of conflict. In fact, one can possess inner peace even when the storms of conflict swirl about him. Inner peace is not determined by circumstances but by the indwelling Holy Spirit who keeps our minds and hearts close to Christ Jesus. *Shalom* is peace, the fullness of life, and all the abundance and prosperity that a peaceful life possesses in Christ.

The Holy Spirit also brings peace among people. "Always keep yourselves united in the Holy Spirit, and bind yourselves together with peace" (Eph. 4:3). Unity in the Spirit brings peace.

In what areas of your life do you need to know the peace that only the Spirit can give? Check the areas of your mind which need to be controlled by the Spirit's peace:

❑ Making choices   ❑ Attitudes

❑ Feelings   ❑ Anger

❑ Habits   ❑ Jealousy

❑ Envy   ❑ Worry

❑ Fear

❑ Other: _____

Paul writes, "Don't worry about anything; instead, pray about everything. Tell God what you need, and thank him for all he has done. If you do this, you will experience God's peace, which is far more wonderful than the human mind can understand. His peace will guard your hearts and minds as you live in Christ Jesus" (Phil. 4:6–7).

Perhaps you have expected the Holy Spirit to make every situation in your life peaceful and calm. Change your expectations. The Holy Spirit gives you peace in the midst of every situation.

> *We have trials and difficulties in this world, but the peace of Christ through His Spirit overcomes every trial and sorrow (John 16:12–33).*

You have His peace through His indwelling Spirit in the middle of every one of life's storms. Read Isaiah 26:3 and then rewrite or paraphrase it in your own words:

_____

_____

_____

Write a prayer asking God's Spirit to control your mind with His peace:

_____

_____

_____

_____

_____

A nd when he [the Holy Spirit] comes, he will convince the world of its sin, and of God's righteousness, and of the coming judgment. The world's sin is unbelief in me (John 16:8–9).

The beguiling subtlety of sin is denial. Sin's addiction desires to cover up every sin. So our sin denies that we sin. But God's truth uncovers our sinfulness. "If we say we have no sin, we are only fooling ourselves and refusing to accept the truth. . . . If we claim we have not sinned, we are calling God a liar and showing that his word has no place in our hearts" (1 John 1:8, 10).

If denial reinforces sin's addiction, then confession will break sin's hold on us. "But if we confess our sins to him, he is faithful and just to forgive us and to cleanse us from every wrong" (1 John 1:9).

Below is a list of some common sins. On the left, rank the sins in the order of their frequency in your life. On the right, rank from the most difficult (1) to the least difficult (11) sin to repent of and confess.

Frequency	Sins	Difficult to confess
_____	Jealousy	_____
_____	Hate	_____
_____	Lust	_____
_____	Pride	_____
_____	Gossip	_____
_____	Idolatry	_____
_____	Disrespect	_____
_____	Rebellion	_____
_____	Being judgmental	_____
_____	Causing conflict	_____
_____	Other:_____	_____

The Holy Spirit exposes our sin. He is the Spirit of truth. Truth never condones the lies of denial prompted by our addiction to sin.

God's Spirit exposes the world's sin of unbelief. When a person chooses not to trust in Christ as Lord and Savior, the Spirit exposes that sin. Likewise, the Holy Spirit inspires the faith within us to confess Jesus as Lord. "So I want you to know how to discern what is truly from God: No one speaking by the Spirit of God can curse Jesus, and no one is able to say, 'Jesus is Lord'—except by the Holy Spirit" (1 Cor. 12:3).

> *If there is any area in your life in which you do not totally trust Jesus, the Holy Spirit will reveal it and bring conviction to your heart.*

One of the most powerful passages in all of Scripture describing the convicting power of the Spirit is Psalm 51—David's prayer after committing adultery. If the Holy Spirit is convicting you of sin in any area of your life at this moment, pray this prayer aloud, putting your name in each blank.

"Have mercy on _____ , O God, because of Your unfailing love. Because of Your great compassion, blot out the stain of_____'s sins. Wash _____ clean from my guilt. Purify_____ from my sin. Don't keep looking at _____'s sins. Remove the stain of_____'s guilt. Create in _____ a clean heart, O God. Renew a right spirit within _____. Do not banish_____ from Your presence, and don't take Your Holy Spirit from_____." Amen.

*R*ighteousness is available because I go to the Father, and you will see me no more (John 16:10).

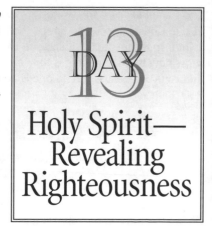

DAY 13

Holy Spirit—
Revealing
Righteousness

The Holy Spirit reveals the righteousness of God through the crucifixion and resurrection of Jesus Christ. Righteousness is more than doing what's right—it is being right with God through faith in Christ. The Holy Spirit convinces the world that there is none righteous except God. "For no one can ever be made right in God's sight by doing what his law commands. For the more we know God's law, the clearer it becomes that we aren't obeying it" (Rom. 3:20).

Look up each of the following passages and jot down what it says about righteousness:

Jeremiah 17:9 _____

Genesis 15:6 _____

Psalm 11:7_____

Psalm 85:10–13 _____

Romans 5:18_____

1 Timothy 3:16 _____

The only righteous person ever to live was Christ. The Holy Spirit revealed Him to be righteous (1 Tim. 3:16) and imputes His righteousness to us. Jesus declares, "Righteousness is available because I go to the Father, and you will see me no more" (John 16:10). He sends His Holy Spirit to us and imparts to us His righteousness.

In order to have a right relationship with God, we need the righteousness of Jesus Christ. We cannot be righteous in our own efforts. But by faith in Christ, we receive His righteousness.

Read Romans 5:1–2 and then answer these questions:

❖ What makes us right in God's sight?_____

❖ Why do we have peace? _____

❖ What position do we now enjoy in Christ? _____

❖ What do we look forward to in Christ? _____

> *When we try in our own strength to do what's right,*
> *we fail and become frustrated with ourselves. But*
> *when we trust Christ to work His righteousness in us*
> *by His Spirit, we overcome sin and defeat Satan.*

In the power of the Holy Spirit, Christians can live righteous lives (1 John 3:1–8). Jesus' righteousness destroys the works of the devil in our lives. Complete these sentences:

❖ Through Christ's righteousness, the Spirit has destroyed_____

_____ in my life.

❖ I have a right relationship with God because_____

_____.

Write a prayer thanking Christ for His righteousness and asking Him to work His righteousness in you by the power of His Holy Spirit:

_____

_____

_____

_____

_____

*J*udgment will come because the prince of this world has already been judged (John 16:11).

To judge *(krino)* is to assign an eternal destiny to someone. Judgment passes a sentence of innocent or guilty. Only the Holy Spirit can judge a person's life. Jesus warns, "Stop judging others, and you will not be judged" (Matt. 7:1).

The Holy Spirit has already revealed the coming judgment of the prince of this world, Satan. In the vision the Spirit gave to John in Revelation, we read that "the Devil, who betrayed them, was thrown into the lake of fire that burns with sulfur, joining the beast and the false prophet. There they will be tormented day and night forever and ever" (Rev. 20:10).

So we know the enemy's judgment—eternal torment in the lake of fire. Since the Spirit has already revealed Satan's destiny, why do you fear his attacks? He is already defeated. Read for yourself and jot down the future of the enemy and the power you have in the Spirit over him:

Luke 10:18–19 _____

Romans 16:20 _____

Ephesians 6:11 _____

Hebrews 2:14 _____

James 4:7 _____

1 John 2:13–14 _____

1 John 3:8 _____

Revelation 12:10 _____

Now read 1 John 4:4. Describe in your own words an encounter you have had with the enemy in which he was soundly defeated by the power of God's Spirit within you:

_____

_____

_____

> *The Spirit of God has judged and condemned Satan.*

Still the enemy tries to attack and accuse us so that we will be powerless to resist him. While he may accuse us of past sins, they have been forgiven and cleansed by the blood of Jesus Christ. Satan has no authority to judge us. Rather, he is judged, pronounced guilty, and condemned.

What then is the position of those who walk in the Spirit? Read each passage and write down your present and future in Christ:

The Word	My Present	My Future in Christ
John 3:16		
John 10:10		
John 11:25–26		
Romans 5:3–11		
Romans 10:9–13		
Ephesians 1:3–14		
Colossians 3:1–15		
Revelation 21:1–7		

Write a prayer giving praise to Christ for defeating Satan and giving you the Holy Spirit to defeat the enemy daily:

_____

_____

_____

_____

_____

*W*hen the Spirit of truth comes, he will guide you into all truth. He will not be presenting his own ideas; he will be telling you what he has heard. He will tell you about the future (John 16:13).

DAY 15
Holy Spirit— Revealing the Future

In Christ, your future is secure. The Holy Spirit has revealed your future as a believer in the Word of God. In fact, the Spirit of God has been given to you to guarantee your future, "The Spirit is God's guarantee that he will give us everything he promised and that he has purchased us to be his own people" (Eph. 1:14).

Right now, how are you really feeling about your future? Circle all the feelings you have about your future:

Hopeful	Anxious	Expectant	Worried
Optimistic	Pessimistic	Joyful	Blessed
Fearful	Excited	Apprehensive	Sad

Other:_____

The Holy Spirit creates hope within us for the future.

His indwelling presence fills us with God's love, which continually reassures us and gives us confidence. God's Spirit is at work in us to ground and root us in hope. We may not entirely know what the future holds, but we do know *who* holds the future. In God's hands, our future is safe and secure.

Spirit-led believers look forward to the future even when it may be filled with problems and trials. Why? How is that possible? Look closely at Romans 5:1–5. Now take this short True or False Quiz based on Romans 5.

True or False (Mark *T* for True and *F* for False before each statement.)

_____ 1. We are righteous as a result of living a good life.

_____ 2. When we trust in Christ, He raises us up to a place of highest privilege.

_____ 3. We can joyfully look forward to God's future for us.

_____ 4. The believer's future will be free of trials and problems.

_____ 5. Difficulties ruin faith.

_____ 6. Problems never defeat a Christian—they simply strengthen a

believer's character.

_____ 7. We can be confident of our salvation.

_____ 8. God's Spirit fills us with His love and expectant hope.

The Holy Spirit has already revealed the nature of God's plans for our future. Read Jeremiah 29:11–12. Paraphrase that passage in your own words:

_____

_____

_____

Jesus is preparing a place for us and coming back for us (John 14). So in expectation of God's future for us, "The Spirit and the bride [Christ's church] say, 'Come.' Let each one who hears them say, 'Come.' Let the thirsty ones come—anyone who wants to. Let them come and drink the water of life without charge" (Rev. 22:17).

Write a prayer thanking God for the future He has revealed by His Spirit for you:

_____

_____

_____

_____

_____

*H*e [the Spirit of truth] will bring me glory by revealing to you whatever he receives from me. All that the Father has is mine; this is what I mean when I say that the Spirit will reveal to you whatever he receives from me (John 16:14–15).

Day 16

Holy Spirit— Revealing Jesus

The person of the Holy Spirit never draws attention to Himself. His sole purpose is to draw us to Jesus so that we hear and receive whatever Jesus has for us.

The closer we get to the Holy Spirit, the more we will know about Jesus. The more we receive from the Spirit, the more we will have from Jesus. For example, the gifts of the Holy Spirit are really the ministry of Jesus being implemented in His body, the church (1 Cor. 12–14). And the gifts of the Holy Spirit are really the nature and likeness of Jesus Christ being produced in us (Gal. 5:22–23).

So if you want to see, know, and grow intimate with Jesus, let the Holy Spirit reveal Him to you. If you want to know how the Holy Spirit will work in your life, then study the life of Jesus.

Each passage below reveals something about the relationship between Jesus and the Holy Spirit. Read each passage and then jot down a brief phrase that describes what the Spirit did in and through Jesus.

Matthew 1:18 _____

Matthew 3:11–12 _____

Matthew 4:1 _____

Luke 4:14–18 _____

Matthew 12:18 _____

Luke 10:21 _____

Romans 8:11 _____

> *Consider this: The same Holy Spirit that raised Jesus from the dead has raised you from the death of your sins and given you new life.*

Has the Spirit been revealing Jesus in power and ministry to your life? Read John 14:12. Now put an *x* on the line, marking how you have encountered Jesus through the Spirit at work in you:

1. The Holy Spirit conceived Jesus. He has also birthed new life in me.

_____

This I have encountered.   I have not encountered this yet.

2. The Holy Spirit confirmed Jesus as the Son of God at baptism. I have been baptized and know that I am God's child.

_____

This I have encountered.   I have not encountered this yet.

3. The Holy Spirit led Jesus into the wilderness. God's Spirit has led me through deserts and helped me resist temptations.

_____

This I have encountered.   I have not encountered this yet.

4. The Holy Spirit anointed and used Jesus powerfully for ministry. He has also anointed me and uses me powerfully for ministry.

_____

This I have encountered.   I have not encountered this yet.

Write a prayer asking the Holy Spirit to work and minister through you as He did through Jesus:

_____

_____

_____

_____

_____

A *nd everyone present was filled with the Holy Spirit and began speaking in other languages [other tongues], as the Holy Spirit gave them this ability (Acts 2:4).*

At Pentecost, the Holy Spirit poured out His power upon the church. This fulfilled the prophecy given by God through Joel the prophet. Read Joel 2:28–32 and complete each prophetic statement:

DAY 17

Encounter His Power to Speak

❖ Your sons and daughters will _____

_____.

❖ Your young men will_____.

❖ Your old men will _____.

❖ Servants, men, and women alike will _____.

❖ Anyone who calls upon the name of the Lord will_____.

The Holy Spirit empowers us to speak in other languages so that others may hear, understand, and receive the gospel of Jesus Christ. When the Holy Spirit spoke through the early Christians in Acts 2:1–13, how did others respond? Read these verses and list their reponses:

❖ Acts 2:6_____

❖ Acts 2:7–8 _____

❖ Acts 2:11 _____

❖ Acts 2:12 _____

Check the ways you have encountered the Holy Spirit speaking *through* you or *to* you:

❑ Other tongues or languages   ❑ Prophecy

❑ Visions   ❑ Dreams

❑ Spirit-inspired preaching   ❑ Interpretation of tongues

❑ Scripture   ❑ His voice in my heart

❑ Other: _____

The Holy Spirit baptizes and fills His people to speak boldly the Word of God. His baptism comes as a purifying, purging, cleansing fire.

Read Matthew 3:11–12; Luke 3:15–18; and Acts 2:1–4. In your own words, describe the fiery baptism of God's Spirit:

_____

_____

_____

Ask yourself:

❖ Has the Holy Spirit spoken through you?

❖ Are you listening for His voice?

❖ What dreams, visions, and prophecy has He poured out upon you to share with others?

Write a prayer thanking Jesus for baptizing you with His Spirit and fire, and for speaking powerfully through you with boldness:

_____

_____

_____

_____

_____

A *deep sense of awe came over them all, and the apostles performed many miraculous signs and wonders (Acts 2:43).*

After Pentecost, the Holy Spirit worked mightily through the lives of the apostles and early believers. They saw many miracles, signs, and wonders wrought by the Holy Spirit in their midst.

Jesus had promised that "when the Holy Spirit has come upon you, you will receive power and will tell people about me anywhere" (Acts 1:7).

DAY 18

Encounter His Power to Work Miracles

Take a survey of the Book of Acts to see the Spirit's mighty works of power. Read each scripture below and write down the manifestation of the Spirit's power that was revealed:

The Text	The Spirit's Power
Acts 4:8	
Acts 4:31	
Acts 5:1–16	
Acts 6:1–7	
Acts 7:54–60	
Acts 8:1–25	
Acts 8:26–40	
Acts 9:1–19	
Acts 9:31	
Acts 10:44–48	
Acts 11:24	
Acts 12:1–12	
Acts 13:52	
Acts 16:6–10	
Acts 19:1–7	

The Holy Spirit gifts members of the body of Christ to work miracles and heal the sick (1 Cor. 12:1–11). What power encounters have you witnessed? In what ways have you seen the Holy Spirit work? Check all those that you have witnessed and underline those through which the Spirit has used you as the instrument of His power:

❑ Healing the sick   ❑ Working miracles

❑ Casting out devils   ❑ Having prophetic words

❑ Interpreting tongues

❑ Speaking in tongues and other languages

❑ Ministering in the gifts of the Holy Spirit

❑ Other:_____

Are you allowing the Holy Spirit to minister through you with His power? How do you respond to the power of the Holy Spirit? Circle the responses you have had to the Spirit's desire to use you:

Willing	Receptive	Open
Afraid	Excited	Thankful
Available	Resistive	

Other: _____

> *If you are not open to the power of the Holy Spirit flowing into and through your life, what within you is resisting the Holy Spirit?*

Identify any resistance you have to the Holy Spirit and surrender it to His control. Paul writes, "But you are not controlled by your sinful nature. You are controlled by the Spirit if you have the Spirit of God living in you" (Rom. 8:9). What must you do to surrender control to the Holy Spirit?

Write a prayer asking Jesus to fill you with the miracle-working power of the Spirit:

_____

_____

_____

*A*ll the people saw him walking and heard him praising God. When they realized he was the lame beggar they had seen so often at the Beautiful Gate, they were absolutely astounded! They all rushed out to Solomon's Colonnade, where he was holding tightly to Peter and John. Everyone stood there in awe of the wonderful thing that had happened (Acts 3:9–11).

Encounter His Power to Heal

By the power of the Holy Spirit, Peter ministered healing to the crippled man at the temple. The gift of healing from the Holy Spirit is available to the body of Christ. "A spiritual gift is given to each of us as means of helping the entire church. . . . The Spirit gives special faith to another, and to someone else he gives the power to heal the sick" (1 Cor. 12:7, 9).

The power to heal resides with the Holy Spirit and not with the vessel He uses to heal. Peter and John did not heal the crippled man—God did. Yet, God still needs willing and obedient human vessels to minister healing through the Holy Spirit's power.

Do you believe that God can and does still heal today? Check your position for each of the following statements:

	Witnessed	Believe	Not Sure	No Way
God physically heals today.	❏	❏	❏	❏
God heals emotions today.	❏	❏	❏	❏
God heals spiritually today.	❏	❏	❏	❏
God only heals through medicine.	❏	❏	❏	❏
God heals naturally and supernaturally today.	❏	❏	❏	❏
God uses me to minister His healing power.	❏	❏	❏	❏

There is no indication in Scripture that the healing power of the Holy Spirit ceased after the apostolic era. In fact, church history records countless healings by the Spirit's power throughout the centuries. So, why is it that we do not experience His healing power being abundantly manifested throughout His body today? Put in rank order the reasons you believe God's healing is hindered today:

_____ Lack of biblical teaching and understanding

_____ Lack of faith

_____ Lack of available and willing people to minister the Holy Spirit's power

_____ Unbelief in the Spirit's power to heal

_____ Sin and a lack of holiness in the church

_____ Other: _____

> *The Holy Spirit is completely sovereign. That means all healing comes from God and is controlled by His Spirit. We cannot manipulate God or command Him to heal.*

God desires that we be in good health. Read these passages and jot down what the Scripture teaches about His healing power:

Exodus 15:26 _____

Psalm 103:3 _____

Psalm 107:20 _____

Isaiah 53:4–5 _____

Mark 2:40–45 _____

1 Peter 2:24 _____

3 John 2 _____

Write a prayer asking Jesus to use you as a vessel of His healing whenever He wills:

_____

_____

_____

_____

_____

*T*hen Saul, also known as Paul, filled with the Holy Spirit, looked at the sorcerer in the eye and said, "You son of the Devil, full of every sort of trickery and villainy; enemy of all that is good, will you never stop perverting the ways of the Lord?" (Acts 13:9–10).

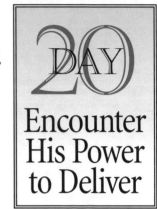

Encounter His Power to Deliver

The Holy Spirit gives us the power and boldness to confront the enemy. At times, the enemy is simply rebuked and defeated as in this passage from Acts 13. At other times, a person is completely delivered from bondage (Acts 16:16–21). At other times, the demon is sent packing in the name of Jesus, as in the case in Philippi when a demon-possessed girl following Paul around was told by Paul, "'I command you in the name of Jesus Christ to come out of her'. . . Instantly it left her" (Acts 16:18).

The Holy Spirit powerfully delivers people from demons and devils in the name of Jesus. This work of the Spirit is called *deliverance.* This power manifestation of the Spirit simply illustrates the truth of 1 John 4:4, "Because the Spirit who lives in you is greater than the spirit who lives in the world."

Believers are not possessed by demons—they are possessed by God (1 Peter 2:9). Believers may be oppressed, attacked, and harassed by demons, but only those who do not believe are possessed. How does the Spirit set people free? Empowered by the Holy Spirit (Luke 4:14–15), Jesus taught about demons and delivered people. Read each scripture from the Gospel of Luke and write down what people are delivered from and how they are delivered:

Delivered	From What?	How?
Luke 4:41		
Luke 8:26–39		
Luke 9:49–50		
Luke 10:18–20		
Luke 11:14–28		
Luke 13:10–17		

Deliverance is a power encounter with the Holy Spirit. The powers of darkness are confronted by the light of God's Spirit and must flee (Eph. 4:17–24; 2 Cor. 11).

Deliverance is not something the believer does. He or she is simply an obedient vessel of the Holy Spirit, who does the actual deliverance. All believers have been delivered: "For he [God] has rescued us from the one who rules in the kingdom of darkness, and he has brought us into the Kingdom of his dear Son. God has purchased our freedom with his blood and has forgiven all our sins" (Col. 1:13–14).

List at least five things Jesus has delivered you from, and also list what replaced them:

Jesus Delivered Me From . . .	He Gave Me . . .
1.	
2.	
3.	
4.	
5.	

The power of His Spirit not only *sets* us free, He *keeps* us free. No longer are we in bondage to the Law. We are free in the Spirit to live by faith. "So Christ has really set us free. Now make sure that you stay free, and don't get tied up again in slavery to the law. . . . But we who live by the Spirit eagerly wait to receive everything promised to us who are right with God through faith" (Gal. 5:1, 5).

Write a prayer asking Jesus to use you as a vessel of His deliverance whenever He wills:

_____

_____

_____

_____

*N*ow there are different kinds of spiritual gifts, but it is the same Holy Spirit who is the source of them all. There are different kinds of service in the church, but it is the same Lord that we are serving. There are different ways God works in our lives, but it is the same God who does the work through all of us. A spiritual gift is given to each of us as a means of helping the entire church (1 Cor. 12:4–7).

DAY 21

Encounter the Gifts of the Spirit

The gift of the Holy Spirit in our lives is accompanied by the gifts of the Spirit. He alone distributes the gifts and decides which gift(s) we will receive (see 1 Cor. 12). We cannot manipulate, control, or choose the gifts. The sovereign Holy Spirit gives gifts not according to our wants but according to the needs of the church.

Below is a list of gifts from 1 Corinthians 12, Romans 12, Ephesians 4, and 1 Peter 4. This is not an exhaustive list but simply an overview of the gifts mentioned in these Scripture passages. Check the gift(s) the Spirit has empowered you to minister to the church. Circle the gifts that the Spirit has used through others to minister to you.

❏ Power to heal the sick

❏ Wise advice

❏ Teaching

❏ Ability to perform miracles

❏ Apostle

❏ Serving others

❏ Ability to lead

❏ Showing kindness

❏ Pastoring

❏ Ability to prophesy

❏ Special knowledge

❏ Helping others

❏ Faith

❏ Getting others to work together

❏ Encouraging

❏ Giving generously

❏ Evangelizing

❏ Preaching

❏ Ability to discern the Spirit of God from other spirits

❏ Ability to speak in tongues (unknown languages)

❏ Ability to interpret tongues (unknown languages)

*The Spirit of God gives gifts to the saints for equipping and minister-
ing to one another in the body of Christ and for demonstrating the
power of God in Christ to unbelievers. Gifts are never to be used for
comparison with other believers or for personal gain and glory.*

When we encounter the Holy Spirit ministering His gifts, we encounter the ministry of Jesus Christ through His body, the church. In the same ways He ministered in His earthly ministry, His body ministers now through the power of the
Spirit.

Describe a time when someone ministered to you through a gift of the Spirit:

_____

_____

Describe a time when you ministered to another person through a gift of the
Spirit.

_____

_____

*Write a prayer seeking the ministry of the Spirit's gifts through you to
others:*

_____

_____

_____

_____

_____

*G*od has given each of us the ability to do certain things well. So if God has given you the ability to prophesy, speak out when you have faith that God is speaking through you. If your gift is that of serving others, serve them well. If you are a teacher, do a good job of teaching. If your gift is to encourage others, do it! If you have money, share it generously. If God has given you leadership ability, take the responsibility seriously. And if you have a gift for showing kindness to others, do it gladly (Rom. 12:6–8).

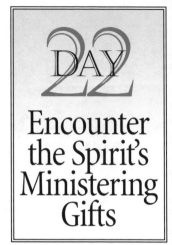

DAY 22

Encounter the Spirit's Ministering Gifts

Some of the many gifts for ministry are described in Romans 12. The word *ministry (diakoneo)* means "to serve or take care of." Deacons were chosen in the early church to minister to the needs of the saints (Acts 6). The Holy Spirit empowers us to minister to the needs of others through His gifts.

Carefully examine this list of ministry gifts from Romans 12. Put an *x* on the line describing how each gift is being used in your church.

Ministry Gifts	Used Often	Rarely Used
Prophecy	_____	_____
Serving others	_____	_____
Teaching	_____	_____
Encouragement	_____	_____
Sharing money	_____	_____
Leadership	_____	_____
Showing kindness	_____	_____

Which of the above gifts has the Spirit ministered *through* you? _____

To you? _____

If some of these ministry gifts are lacking in your life or your church, something may be hindering them. The Spirit is hindered in ministering through His gifts when we get in the way, blocking His power and flow. How do we get in the way?

Below is a list of some of the ways we hinder the flow of ministry through the Spirit's gifts. Circle any hindrances that are in your life or in your church's life:

Pride	Comparison
Fear	Ignorance
Unwillingness to minister	Unbelief
Lack of openness to the Holy Spirit	Unconfessed sin

Other: _____

Each of us is a servant or minister of Christ and servants of others upon whom the Spirit of God is poured out (Acts 2:18). As servants, the Spirit empowers our ministry with His gifts.

> *While Christ may utilize our skills and abilities, His gifts are supernatural abilities that we receive by grace, not by education or effort.*

And when He ministers through us by His Spirit, Christ—not people—receives all glory, praise, and honor.

Write a prayer seeking Christ's ministry gifts to flow through you:

_____

_____

_____

_____

_____

*H*e is the one who gave these gifts to the church: the apostles, the prophets, the evangelists, and the pastors and teachers. Their responsibility is to equip God's people to do his work and build up the church, the body of Christ, until we come to such unity in our faith and knowledge of God's Son that we will be mature and full grown in the Lord, measuring up to the full stature of Christ (Eph. 4:11–13).

Encounter His Equipping Gifts

God's Spirit has gifted ministers in the body of Christ to equip His people for ministry.

❖ *Apostles* go forth with the gospel as missionaries who plant churches and begin new works for Christ.

❖ *Prophets* proclaim and preach God's Word.

❖ *Evangelists* share the Good News of Christ, witnessing to God's salvation in Jesus and leading others to faith in Him.

❖ *Pastors* nurture and care for the sheep in the body of Christ.

❖ *Teachers* disciple and instruct members of the body in the Word of God.

These ministers of the gospel are empowered by God's Spirit to raise up others in the body of Christ to minister to and lead the flock of Christ, and to witness to the world.

Take a moment to thank God for the different people you have known who have equipped you and other members of the body. Throughout history there have been Spirit-filled saints who have equipped the body: Origen, Iraneaus, Tertullian, Augustine, Aquinas, Luther, Calvin, Wesley, Wycliffe, Hus, Seymour, Etter, Kuhlman, Graham, and many others.

In the space below, pray by name for those you know of who are being used by God:

Apostles: _____

Prophets: _____

Evangelists: _____

Pastors: _____

Teachers: _____

> *These fivefold offices of the church are empowered by the Spirit to equip the saints for one purpose— that they become mature in the Lord.*

How is your maturity in Christ? Below are three pie charts representing the three areas of your life. Label four of the areas in each part. The suggested list under each area is just to get you thinking. Shade in each area to the degree that you are mature in Christ.

Spirit	**Soul**	**Body**
Prayer	Will	Eating
Bible study	Attitudes	Appearance
Giving	Thoughts	Desires
Fasting	Feelings	Actions
Worship	Decisions	Habits
Witnessing		

Write a prayer asking for God to bring into your life those gifted by the Holy Spirit to equip and help mature you:

_____

_____

_____

_____

_____

B ut when the Holy Spirit controls our lives, he will produce this kind of fruit in us: love, joy, peace, patience, kindness, goodness, faithfulness, gentleness, and self control. Here there is no conflict with the law (Gal. 5:22–23)

In these final seven days of our study together, we will explore the fruit of the Spirit. Each fruit is a way that the Holy Spirit manifests the likeness of Christ in our lives. The sinful nature produces destructive desires, but those bondages are broken by the power of the Spirit in our lives (Gal. 5:19–21). Those sinful desires are replaced by the fruit of His Spirit.

> *The Holy Spirit produces the fruit of love in our lives. God's love (agape) is to be more desired than all the gifts (1 Cor. 13). His love is unconditional, unmerited favor bestowed upon the one loved.*

The one loved can do nothing to earn or deserve the love received. Likewise, the gift of love is not conditioned upon the merit or the appreciation of the one being loved.

The importance of love in the Christian life cannot be overstated. Read the following passages and jot down what each scripture says about the importance of love:

John 13:34–35 _____

Luke 10:27–28 _____

Luke 14:26 _____

Romans 12:9–10 _____

Romans 13:8 _____

1 Corinthians 13 _____

1 Corinthians 14:1 _____

Galatians 5:6 _____

1 John 4:7–21 _____

So how is your love life in the Spirit? The fruit of love has certain qualities and characteristics that are described in 1 Corinthians 13. Below is a list of those qualities. Examine yourself and position yourself with an *x* on the line of each quality:

(The quality of godly love is in bold.)

Patient   Impatient

Kind   Cruel

Not jealous   Jealous

Not boastful or proud   Proud

Not demanding   Controlling

Not irritable   Irritable

No record of wrongs   Records offenses

Rejoices in the truth   Glad about injustice

Never gives up   Throws in the towel

Lasts forever   Quickly fades

Ask the Holy Spirit to produce the fruit of love in your life:

---

*T*hen Jesus was filled with the joy of the Holy Spirit (Luke 10:21).

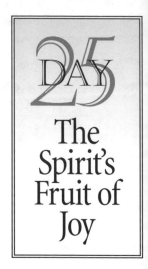

The Spirit's Fruit of Joy

Wherever the Spirit is, there is joy. Again and again, the Scriptures mention the joy that is produced when God's Spirit is present in our lives.

> *Joy is a state of celebration, praise, and blessedness that springs from the Spirit of God. No circumstance or person can steal our joy (John 16:16–33). While happiness is conditioned by what happens to us, joy flows from the One who lives in us—the Holy Spirit.*

Joy springs from the assurance that God's grace and love for us in Christ are unconditional. Joy is our basic response to all of life—even suffering. "So be truly glad! There is wonderful joy ahead, even though it is necessary for you to endure many trials for a while . . . You love him even though you have never seen him. Though you do not see him, you trust him; and even now you are happy with a glorious, inexpressible joy" (1 Pet. 1:6, 8).

Even though imprisoned, Paul is filled with joy when he writes his letter to the Philippians. Take a moment to skim through that letter. List all of Paul's references to joy and rejoicing:

_____

_____

_____

God gives us an abundance of reasons to rejoice. Below is a list of just a few. Read the verses, then jot down the causes of such joy. After you do so, start rejoicing!

Luke 1:47 _____

Romans 5:3, 11 _____

Habbakuk 3:18 _____

Psalm 119:162 _____

Psalm 118:124 _____

Philippians 4:4 _____

Luke 1:14 _____

The Holy Spirit also empowers the blessings of God's kingdom. The Beatitudes in Matthew 5:1–12 are not laws or rules for living but attitudes of being that are rooted in the Spirit of God. Especially joyful are those who recognize their need for God's Spirit (5:3).

How intense is your desire and need for God's Spirit? Shade in the thermometer to represent how hungry you are for God's Spirit. Remember, the greater the hunger, the greater the joy!

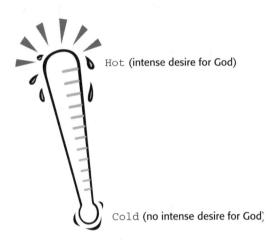

Hot (intense desire for God)

Cold (no intense desire for God)

Write a prayer asking to be filled with the Spirit's joy:

_____

_____

_____

_____

_____

*F*or the Kingdom of God is not a matter of what we eat or drink, but of living a life of goodness and peace and joy in the Holy Spirit (Rom. 14:17).

Goodness, peace, and joy are all found in the Holy Spirit. He is the source of all three. His peace binds the church together in unity. "Always keep yourselves united in the Holy Spirit, and bind yourselves together with peace" (Eph. 4:3).

> *The fruit of peace produces harmony and unity among believers. Those filled with the Spirit do not create division and strife within the body of Christ.*

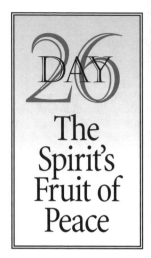

DAY 26

The Spirit's Fruit of Peace

"How wonderful it is, how pleasant, when brothers live together in harmony! For harmony is as precious as the fragrant anointing oil that was poured over Aaron's head, that ran down his beard and onto the border of his robe. Harmony is as refreshing as the dew from Mount Hermon that falls on the mountains of Zion. And the Lord has pronounced his blessing, even life forevermore" (Ps. 133). Throughout Scripture, both anointing oil and water (the refreshing dew) are symbolic of the Holy Spirit. As His Spirit anoints us and washes us, the peace of harmony is produced in our relationships.

Peace—abundant life, blessing, prosperity, well-being, and harmonious unity—issues from the source of His Spirit. Read Acts 9:31. In your own words, paraphrase this passage about peace in the church and how it is produced:

_____

_____

_____

Whenever Jesus appeared to His disciples in a situation that might startle or frighten them, He greeted them with peace (Luke 24:36; John 20:19; 20:26). Jesus promised in John 16 that upon His return to the Father, He would send the gift of the Holy Spirit and peace (John 16:26–27).

As you welcome the Holy Spirit into your life, where do you most need His fruit of peace? Complete these sentences:

I most need peace with those who _____

_____.

I need inner peace for _____

_____.

What brings me the greatest peace is knowing _____

_____.

The greatest peace a human being can ever experience is peace with God. "Therefore, since we have been made right in God's sight by faith, we have peace with God because of what Jesus Christ our Lord has done for us" (Rom. 5:1). Describe the time in your life when you first had peace with God:

_____

_____

_____

Write a prayer asking to become a peacemaker through the power of the Holy Spirit:

_____

_____

_____

_____

_____

*W*e have proved ourselves by our purity, our understanding, our patience, our kindness, our sincere love, and the power of the Holy Spirit (2 Cor. 6:6).

The Holy Spirit produces the fruit of purity, understanding, kindness, love, and patience in our lives. How powerful are each of these qualities! Take a brief self-test. Put an *x* on the line where you are right now.

In the power of the Holy Spirit, I am . . .

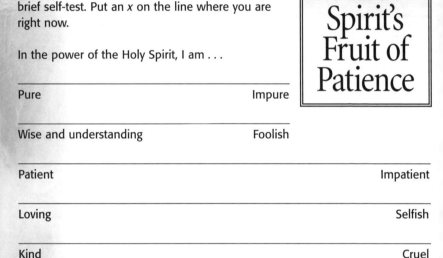

Pure _____ Impure

Wise and understanding _____ Foolish

Patient _____ Impatient

Loving _____ Selfish

Kind _____ Cruel

In what areas that are not yet producing His fruit in power do you need to surrender complete control to the Holy Spirit? Will you surrender now?

> *Patience waits on God's timing and does not push human timetables and desires. Patience does not get ahead of God.*

Patience knows, "But those who wait on the Lord will find new strength. They will fly high on wings like eagles. They will run and not grow weary. They will walk and not faint" (Isa. 40:31).

Where in your life do you most need to be waiting patiently upon the Lord instead of pushing ahead in your own strength and desires? On the next page are the wings of an eagle. Write on the wings the areas in which you need to be waiting upon the Lord:

At times it is difficult to wait. Consider the potter (Jer. 18). There is a season of time in which the potter sets a pot upon a shelf so it can cure and then be ready for the fire. Has God's Spirit put you on the shelf? Are you in a time of waiting, growing, learning, and preparation before He uses you in ministry? How do you handle waiting? Circle the feelings or responses you usually have when you have to wait upon God:

Peace	Restlessness	Worry
Calm	Anxiety	Hopefulness
Steadfastness	Frustration	Joy

Other:_____

If you have negative feelings toward God when you are called upon to be patient, then turn to the Holy Spirit. Ask Him to replace your negative responses with the fruit of His patience.

Ask the Holy Spirit to produce His patience in your life:

_____

_____

_____

_____

_____

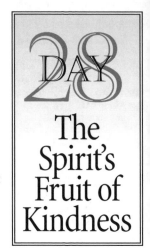

A nd do not bring sorrow to God's Holy Spirit by the way you live. Remember, he is the one who has identified you as his own, guaranteeing that you will be saved on the day of redemption. Get rid of all bitterness, rage, anger, harsh words, and slander, as well as all types of malicious behavior. Instead, be kind to each other, tenderhearted, forgiving one another, just as God through Christ has forgiven you (Eph. 4:30–32).

The Spirit's fruit of kindness produces forgiveness in our lives. Kindness does not hold onto an offense. It is slow to speak in anger and quick to listen. Read each of these scriptures, and jot down what they say about kindness and being slow to anger:

Nehemiah 9:17–21 _____

Proverbs 15:18 _____

Proverbs 16:32 _____

Nahum 1:3 _____

Colossians 1:10 _____

2 Timothy 2:24 _____

Kindness honors and esteems others above ourselves.

Those seeking glory and fame push others out of the way or trample them underfoot. Unkind people have never learned that others treat them the way they treat others. Sowing seeds of kindness reaps a harvest of kindness. Paul writes, "And if you have a gift for showing kindness to others, do it gladly. Don't just pretend that you love others. Really love them. Hate what is wrong. Stand on the side of good. Love each other with genuine affection, and take delight in honoring each other" (Rom. 12:8–10).

Bring to mind five people whom you need to be kind to right now, and list what you need to do to show kindness to each person:

People I need to be kind to: **What I need to do to show kindness:**

_____   _____

_____   _____

People I need to be kind to:	What I need to do to show kindness:
_____	_____
_____	_____
_____	_____

What stifles the fruit of kindness in your life? What dams up the flow of the milk of kindness from the Holy Spirit through you to others? Prioritize, from the greatest hindrance to the least, those things that stop the Spirit's kindness from flowing out of you into the lives of others.

_____ Anger

_____ Hurt

_____ Unforgiveness

_____ Laziness

_____ Forgetfulness

_____ Ingratitude

_____ Selfishness

_____ Other:_____

Now ask the Holy Spirit to remove anything from your life that keeps the fruit of His kindness from growing abundantly in your life.

Ask the Holy Spirit to produce His kindness in your life and to remove every hindrance to kindness.

*F*or the Kingdom of God is not a matter of what we eat or drink, but of living a life of goodness and peace and joy in the Holy Spirit (Rom. 14:17).

DAY 29
The Spirit's Fruit of Goodness

Paul tells those to whom he writes in Rome that they are full of goodness (Rom. 15:14). When we are filled with the Spirit, we are filled with goodness.

The fruit of goodness is God's highest and best life within us. Goodness is filled with mercy and compassion. We know what goodness is because we have a good God. Read each passage about God's goodness and write down a brief summary:

Exodus 33:19 _____

_____

Psalm 31:9_____

Psalm 119:40 _____

Romans 3:5 _____

James 1:17–18 _____

1 Peter 2:9_____

If the Spirit in His goodness desires the best for us and in us, why do we often settle for less than His best? What in you keeps you from producing His goodness? Place a checkmark in each box that applies to you:

❑ Being too hasty to settle for less than the best.

❑ Failing to desire excellence.

❑ Allowing my selfishness to crowd out goodness.

❑ Jealousy over God's goodness in the lives of others.

❑ Failing to yield to the Holy Spirit.

❑ Other:_____

His goodness in you produces a harvest of goodness and peace.

James writes, "And those who are peacemakers will plant seeds of peace and reap a harvest of goodness" (James 3:18). God's goodness at work in us produces a bountiful harvest: Under each grain stalk below, write the kind of harvest you expect when you sow kindness:

List at least five ways you have experienced the fruit of goodness and blessing in your life as the Spirit has ministered to you through others:

1. _____
2. _____
3. _____
4. _____
5. _____

Ask the Holy Spirit to produce the fruit of His goodness in your life.

*S*ome of the brothers recently returned and made me very happy by telling me about your faithfulness and that you are living the truth (3 John 3).

Faithfulness is steadfastness and standing firm on the truth of God. When all else moves, the Spirit-filled soldier of Christ will not be moved. When others compromise the truth, the saint will not be compromised.

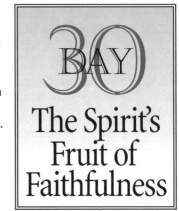

DAY 30
The Spirit's Fruit of Faithfulness

When everyone else is breaking promises, the Spirit within us helps us become promise-keepers.

How does a Spirit-filled believer remain faithful to the Lord and stand firm? Paul writes this: "Be strong with the Lord's mighty power. Put on all of God's armor so that you will be able to stand firm against all strategies and tricks of the Devil" (Eph. 6:10–11).

The armor of God equips the sanctified, Spirit-led believer to produce the fruit of faithfulness. Read Ephesians 6:13–18, and list each part of our spiritual armor. Then indicate which parts of the armor you wear daily. Circle those parts that you most often fail to put on.

1._____

2._____

3._____

4._____

5._____

6._____

You have now surveyed the Scriptures on welcoming the Holy Spirit in your life. You have discovered that by simply asking by faith in Christ, God will give you His Spirit. You have explored the work and ministry of the Holy Spirit in your life. You have also encountered His mighty power at work in the lives of believers. Finally, you uncovered all the different fruit that He is producing in your life as He transforms you from glory to glory into the life of Jesus Christ (2 Cor. 3:18).

To review what you have encountered, complete these sentences:

The most meaningful encounter I had with the Holy Spirit during this devotional study was _____

_____.

One new thing I learned about the Holy Spirit was _____

_____.

Something I need to share with others about the Holy Spirit is _____

_____.

The Holy Spirit ministered most powerfully in my life by _____

_____.

One way the Spirit is using me to minister to others is_____

_____.

The next step I need to take with the Holy Spirit is _____

_____.

Ask the Holy Spirit to take complete control of your life.

You can continue your encounters with the Holy Spirit by using the other devotional study guides listed at the end of this booklet, and by using the companion *Holy Spirit Encounter Bible.*

Leader's Guide

For Group Sessions

This devotional study is an excellent resource for group study including such settings as:

❖ Sunday school classes and other church classes
❖ Prayer groups
❖ Bible study groups
❖ Ministries involving small groups, home groups, and accountability groups
❖ Study groups for youth, men, and women

Before the first session

❖ Contact everyone interested or already participating in the group about the meeting time, date, and place.

❖ Make certain that everyone has a copy of this devotional study guide.

❖ Ask group members to begin their daily encounters in this guide. While each session will not strictly adhere to a seven-day schedule, group members who faithfully do a devotional each day will be prepared to share in the group sessions.

❖ Pray for the Holy Spirit to guide, teach, and help each participant.

❖ Be certain that the place where you will meet has a chalkboard, white board, or flipchart with appropriate writing materials. It is also best to be in a setting with movable, not fixed, seating.

Leader's Guide

Session 1—Welcome the Spirit's Presence

1. Welcome group members as they arrive.

2. Open with a prayer asking God to send His Holy Spirit.

3. On a chalkboard or flipchart, write down group members' responses to this question: "What one word would you use to describe the Holy Spirit?"

4. Ask different group members to read these passages aloud: Luke 11:19–13 and John 14:15–31.

5. Invite anyone who volunteers to share a recent encounter he or she has had with the Holy Spirit.

6. On the board or flipchart, title two columns: Born of Water and Born of the Spirit. Discuss as a group what the differences are between being born of water and born of the Spirit from their study on Day 2.

7. Ask everyone to share when they were born again. If anyone has not been born again in the group, share with them about Jesus Christ as Lord and Savior. Invite them to repent of their sins and receive Him as Lord and Savior (Rom. 1:16–17; 3:23; 5:6–11; 6:1–4; 10:9–13; Acts 2:38).

8. As a total group discuss Acts 2:38 and what each person believes is meant by the phrase, *the gift of the Holy Spirit.*

9. Divide into pairs. It is suggested that you keep the same pairs throughout these four sessions. In pairs, share: "What hinders the Holy Spirit from working in my life?" and, "In what area of my life do I need the power of the Holy Spirit?"

10. Ask the partners in the pairs to pray for one another to receive both the gift and the power of the Holy Spirit in their lives.

11. Form a closing prayer circle. Ask for prayer requests. As the group leader, lead in intercession for the requests that have been made.

Leader's Guide

Session 2—Welcome the Spirit's Ministry

1. Welcome group members as they arrive, and begin with prayer.

2. Ask everyone in the group to remember a time when the Holy Spirit comforted, counseled, convicted, or helped them; ask them to share something about that encounter.

3. Invite anyone who wishes to share how the Holy Spirit has used them to comfort others.

4. Read John 14:15–26 in unison as a group. Ask group members to share which verse is most meaningful to them and why.

5. From Day 8 in this devotional study, ask group members to share the different ways they have encountered the guidance of the Holy Spirit.

6. Ask different group members to read aloud these verses: Psalm 143:10; Luke 12:12; John 14:26; and 1 John 2:27. Share as a group how these verses explain the ways the Holy Spirit teaches us.

7. Ask group members to share how they have encountered the teaching ministry of the Spirit.

8. Invite group members to share their one favorite verse from the Bible. Ask them: "How does the Holy Spirit remind you of the Word in your daily walk with God?"

9. Divide into pairs. Ask the partners to turn to Day 11 and to share which areas of their minds most need the Spirit's peace and why.

10. Ask the partners in the pairs to pray for each other to receive the Spirit's peace of mind.

11. As a total group, form a circle and ask everyone to complete this sentence prayer, "Lord Jesus, I ask You to minister to this group through Your Spirit by

_____."

Leader's Guide

Session 3—Welcome the Spirit's Power

1. Welcome the group members and ask everyone who will pray to ask God to send His Holy Spirit to the group in ministry and power.

2. Read Acts 1:7 in unison aloud as a group.

3. As a group share all the different ways that the Holy Spirit manifests His power. Put the list on a board or flipchart.

4. Invite different group members to share their encounters with the Holy Spirit when He has manifested His power.

5. Put these topics on the board: Revealing Sin; Revealing Righteousness; Revealing Judgment; Revealing the Future; and Revealing Jesus. Ask each group member to choose one topic and to share a time when the Holy Spirit revealed that particular area to his or her life.

6. Ask group members to share their own needs or the needs of others for the power of the Holy Spirit to: heal; prophetically speak; anoint with His gifts; deliver; or equip His people. List these needs on the board or flipchart.

7. As a total group spend time praying and interceding for these needs.

8. Spend about ten minutes in prayer seeking for God to speak prophetically to the group. Wait on the Spirit to speak and listen to His voice.

9. Divide into pairs. Ask the partners to share whatever personal needs they have with their partner. Then ask the partners to pray for one another.

10. Form a closing prayer circle. Sing a chorus and give praise to God for sending His Holy Spirit in power.

Leader's Guide

Session 4—Welcome the Spirit's Gifts and Fruit

1. Welcome the group members as they arrive and open in prayer.

2. In unison as a group, read aloud Galatians 5:22–23.

3. Make two columns on the board or flipchart. Label one column Gifts and the other column Fruit. Without looking at their Bibles, ask group members to name as many gifts and fruit as they can remember. Then check the lists against Days 21 and 24.

4. Invite group members to share which gifts the Spirit has used in their own lives both to minister and to be ministered to in different situations.

5. As a group discuss: What hinders the gifts of the Holy Spirit in our own lives? In our church? In our families? In our witnessing to the world?

6. In pairs, share which fruit personally needs to grow the most in each person's life and then pray for one another.

7. Invite any group members desiring a deeper ministry in the gifts of the Spirit to go to the center of the group and be prayed for to receive the ministry of the Spirit's gifts in power.

8. Go around the group and share: "The most meaningful encounter I have had with the Holy Spirit during this study was _____
_____."

9. Close with a prayer circle, thanking God the Father and God the Son for sending the Holy Spirit.

10. Decide as a group if and when you will go through another Holy Spirit Encounter Guide. A list of all the guides is provided at the end of this booklet.

Titles in the Holy Spirit
Encounter Guide Series

Additional Notes

Additional Notes

Additional Notes

Additional Notes

Additional Notes

Pick up these other Holy Spirit Encounter Bible Study Guides and the *Holy Spirit Encounter Bible* from Charisma House . . .

Holy Spirit Encounter Bible
ISBN: 0-88419-468-X
Retail Price: $24.99

The *Holy Spirit Encounter Bible* is an interactive study and devotional Bible for experiencing the Holy Spirit using the popular New Living Translation. With hundreds of scholarly, yet easy-to-understand outlines, articles, daily readings, notes and in-text study guides, you'll discover how to receive the Spirit's manifest presence in your own life and how to impart His life-changing power in ministry to others.

Charisma's Bible Handbook on the Holy Spirit
John Rea
ISBN: 0-88419-566-X
Retail Price: $24.99

As a companion guide to the *Holy Spirit Encounter Bible, Charisma's Bible Handbook on the Holy Spirit* has been written especially for those who lives have been touched by God in the modern spiritual renewal.

HOLY SPIRIT ENCOUNTER GUIDES

Retail Price: $6.99 each

Welcoming the Presence of the Spirit
ISBN: 0-88419-470-1

Flowing in the River of the Spirit
ISBN: 0-88419-474-4

Living the Spirit-Led Life
ISBN: 0-88419-471-X

Receiving the Anointing of the Spirit
ISBN: 0-88419-475-2

Blazing With the Fire of the Spirit
ISBN: 0-88419-472-8

Operating in the Power of the Spirit
ISBN: 0-88419-494-9

Hearing the Voice of the Spirit
ISBN: 0-88419-473-6

Ministering in the Gifts of the Spirit
ISBN: 0-88419-495-7

Charisma®
HOUSE
Books about Spirit-Led Living

To pick up a copy of any of these titles, contact your local Christian bookstore or order online at www.charismawarehouse.com.